Still Growing

Wren

A Writable Life
San Diego

A Writable Life
3796 Curlew Street
San Diego, CA 92103
Website: www.awritablelife.com

First Edition: December 2022

Design by Teagarden Designs
Cover design by Alyssa Noelle Coelho

Library of Congress Control Number: 2022915549

ISBN 979-8-9858701-3-8 Print
ISBN 979-8-9858701-4-5 eBook

For the people who stayed.

Still Growing

This is the story of growing.

It starts with beautiful promises,
but growth isn't always beautiful or easy.
Like life,
growth is messy, sometimes lonely and painfully raw.

But we continue on.
We find the strength in ourselves to overcome,
and we do just that.

We learn —
from the girl in the mirror,
from ourselves,
from the people around us—
and we grow.

And eventually,
one day,
we shall bloom.

Life is messy—
but *I* am still growing,
but *you* are still growing,
but *she* is still growing.

Don't rush growth,
it is after all what allows us to
bloom.

Remember that even flowers need the rain
to grow.

—Wren

Wren 7

She might not have known everything,

She might not have always been strong,

but She was still growing.

Eventually She would bloom.

Wren 8

She might not have known everything

just a girl
in her lonely tower
watching the world spin
without her,

watching the lights
twinkle from afar
wondering if she too
could be a star.

She stared
out at the stars
on the horizon line
wondering
if she could take them in her hand
and hold them close
to her heart
so that she might never
have to let them go.

Wren 11

She was a little girl
walking through old castles,
feeling the weight of a crown
and dreaming of conquering the world.

Wren 12

What a wonderful spectacle
it was
to see the world
so new
and fresh—
to see the world
as if it were untainted—
like it had been washed clean
from a rain storm.

Wren 13

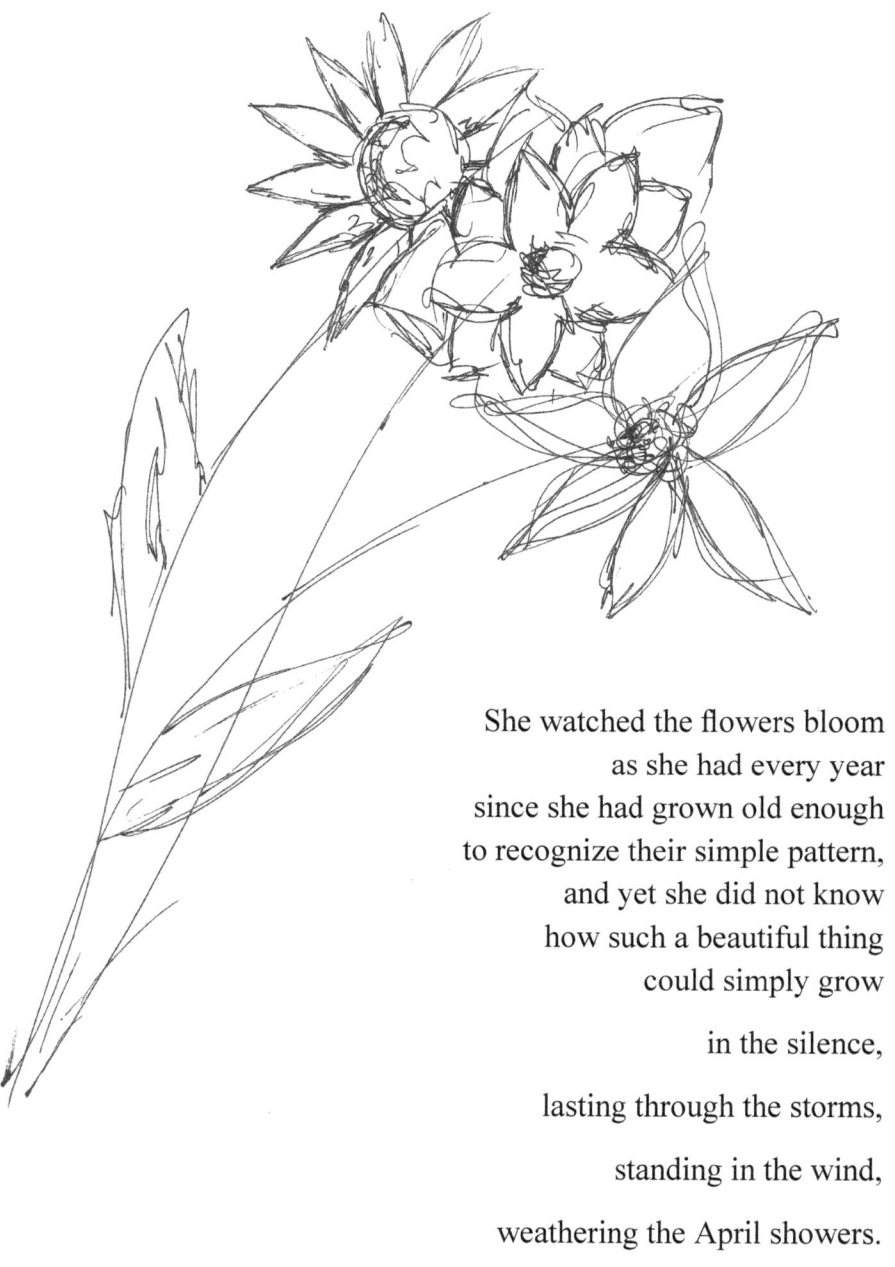

She watched the flowers bloom
as she had every year
since she had grown old enough
to recognize their simple pattern,
and yet she did not know
how such a beautiful thing
could simply grow

in the silence,

lasting through the storms,

standing in the wind,

weathering the April showers.

Wren 14

She planted the seeds
when she was young
so that as she grew old,
she could watch her garden
grow.

Wren 15

It is entirely reasonable
and almost quite commonplace
to look at the stars
and dream of reaching them.

What they deemed unreasonable
and was most certainly not commonplace
was the little girl
who looked at the stars
and began building her rocket.

Wren 16

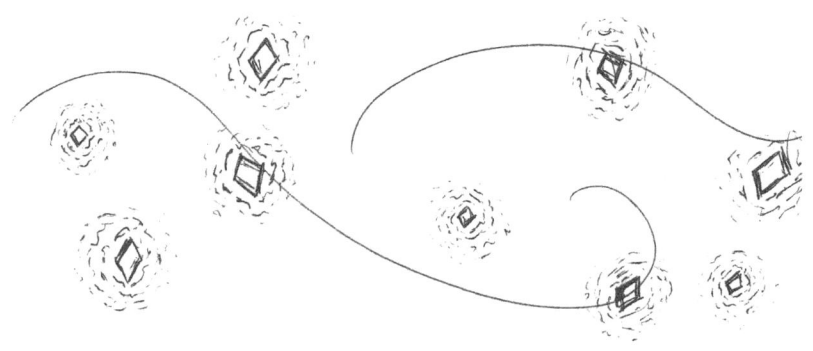

To the starry nights
and the planes that flew across
the horizon—

thank you for showing me
that the world is wider
than I can see.

Thank you for the reminder
to dream.

Wren 17

Traverse the world long enough
and you'll find someone
who will tell you,

"The edge of the world is out there."
They'll whisper it like a secret.

"One day, you'll find it,"
They'll tell you.

"When you're tired,
and yet completely awake,
you'll open your eyes,
and there—
right there,
in between the golden skies,
and the never-ending nights,
where the birds fly,
surrounded by valleys that whisper new melodies
and mountains that echo old songs.

Where life stops you
right in your tracks.
"That,"
They'll whisper,
"That is the beginning
and the end
of everything.
The edge of the world."

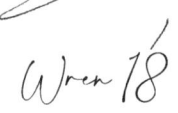

Wren 18

I want to run fast
and I want to run far.

I want to be spontaneous
and free
chasing life
from sea to sea
and from the hills
to the mountains
to the valleys.

I want to explore
this world
on which I live
so that when I grow old,
I am left with
a lifetime
of memories
and a short list of regrets.

I want to fly.

Wren 19

I don't want to be one of those people
who learns too late,
who lives too late,
who watches life pass by.

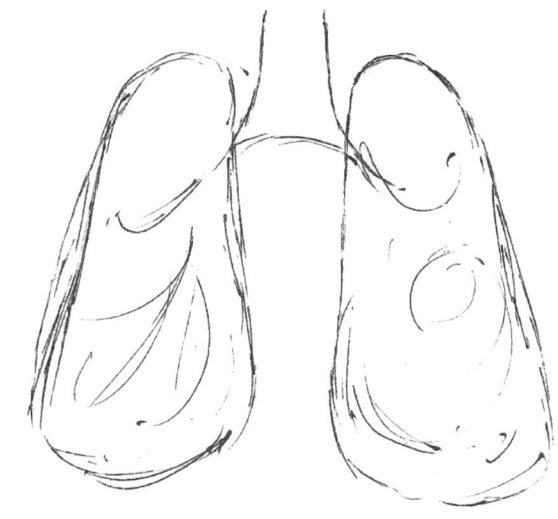

I don't want to be one of those people
who lives their last breath
as though it's their first.

Wren 20

Here I go—

and so I'll run.

Faster.
Further.

I'll run to the stars—
to every corner of this earth.

I will find my dreams
tucked into the universe
waiting for me to take a hold of them,
and so I will.

I will grasp them tightly
and I will never let go again.

Wren 21

As I stare into the unknown,
I am confronted
by the fear of not knowing
what more
could lie beyond
this next step of mine,
and yet I know
that while there could be bad things,
there could be greatness
waiting there too.

Wren 22

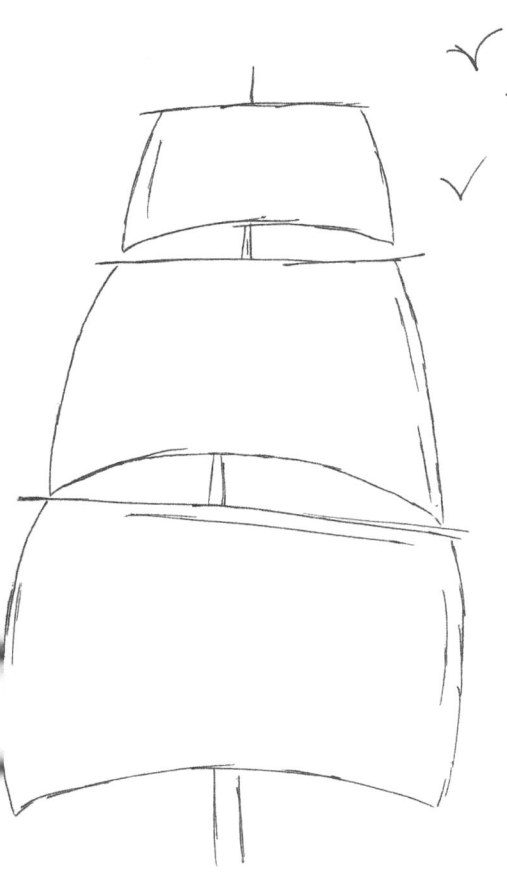

If I am anchored to this shore
by fear,
then I will lift
up my sails
and hold them to the wind.
I will drag in my anchor
and set course
for the horizon

because while fear may be what ties me
to this shore,
I have begun to find the courage
to finally leave the port
and find where this life of mine
may lead me

and so I will follow it
to the stars.

Wren 23

She set sail
for whatever world
lay beyond the edge
of everything she knew.

I found my center
standing on the edge of everything,
at the cross between
living and being afraid,
and here I went

into the great unknown.

Wren 25

Let's set off in search of all we don't know

and leave behind all we do

so that our bags are empty

and our minds are ready

to carry something new.

Wren 26

Her dreams
were far too big
to be kept within the boundaries
of this small town,
And so she left
in search of her dreams
knowing full well
that some of them
were close to impossible,
but also knowing that she had one
very valuable life
she was willing to spend
in the pursuit
of achieving them all.

I love edges—
the lines drawn in the sand,
the borders,
the walls,
the fence between yards
separating the unknown from the known—
the borders of a comfort zone.

I love them because
they show you
exactly when you
step out of that box you call home
and go off on your own
into the great, beautiful
world of the unknown.

Wren 28

What a beautifully, terrifying thing
to stand in front of the horizon line
with the hopes of pinning it down.

What a beautifully, terrifying thing
to dream of catching the winds of
the unknown in your sails
and setting your course for the stars.

Wren 29

She believed in tomorrow.
In the beautiful,
untouched masterpiece
ready to be created.

Wren 30

She pulled her paints
and lay them before her blank canvas.

Finally,
she began,
with one simple stroke,

and she started to paint
the universe.

Wren 31

Watch
as I build wings
from these dreams of mine
and throw myself from a cliff
as I learn to fly.

I hope
that wherever you end up
in this life,
that you are happy.

I hope you find
everything you want
beyond that line.

I hope you wish upon the stars
and find yourself in the sky.

I hope then,
you know
that you have finally learned
to fly—
to shine,

and I hope
it is everything
you dreamed of
from that window of yours.

Wren 33

She left
because
she could not stay
any longer.

She left
because
there was a world
out there
that was calling her name.

She left
because
she had to go.

The stars were waiting
and the tide
was pulling away,
and so she sailed
into the unknown.

Wren 34

She might not have always been strong

The idea
of holding a star in her hand,
of catching and pinning down greatness
lived so vividly behind her eyes,
and yet in every beat of her heart,
she was afraid—
afraid that she might reach up
in that final moment
and miss.

She was afraid
of falling
as Icarus had
as he reached for the sun.

"I'm afraid," She whispered to the echoing silence.
"Of what?" They asked in return.
"Of trying, of caring, of loving something so much…

and failing regardless."

Wren 37

She stopped
at the crossroads
with one path leading forward
and one leading her back
to the safety of her home.

One road
to the beautiful future
and one
to the simple past.

She wanted to turn and run
back to the world she had known,
too afraid
that she would not survive
in this new world
she didn't know.

But the ghosts pushed her forward
even though
she was afraid
she would not be ready.

Wren 38

She stood on the edge
and looked over the side.
It was a long way down,
and she didn't trust the wings
on her back—
Wings carved
from hope,
but tainted by fear—
and so she stood
safely on her cliff,
missing out on the life
that was out there,
just an inch over
the cliff's edge—

and then she fell
like the stars
from the heavens,
grasping for the dark hand
that had forced her off.

Wren 39

When I look up,
I find that I no longer understand
the words
written on this map of mine.

The dreams
I once held so tightly
only remain
as fragments in my mind.

I am a trespasser
in a foreign land.

I don't belong here,
on this road
that has led me so far
from where I was meant to go.

Wren 40

I feel like a bird
who had been kicked out of the nest too early,
but if I had gotten to choose,
would I ever be ready?

Wren 41

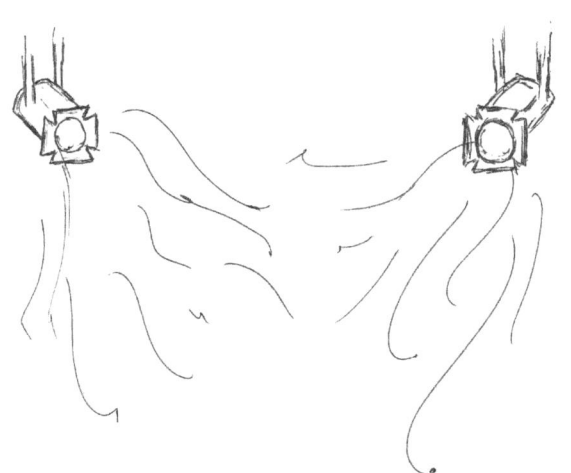

I was thrown out
into the world
and stripped bare
for everyone to see
the raw truth
of my soul.

I was afraid
of what they would find
as they stared.

Was I enough for them?
Would I ever be enough?

I know
we're supposed to love ourselves
and find the greatness within,
but somedays I struggle
to see that shine.
I'm human after all—

I fall apart sometimes.

Wren 43

She ran herself ragged
trying to prove
that she was great,
trying to prove to someone,
to anyone,
to herself,
that she was someone
worthy of attention
and love.

As she set herself on fire
trying to show them how she shined,
she forgot to remember
that she had already been great,
whether or not
someone else saw it.

Wren 44

Far too many times
she had been
the willing victim
of her own doubt.

She stared in the mirror
and picked
at every freckle on her nose,
every strand of hair
that strayed from its proper place,
chasing this idea of being perfect.

Perfect—so that they would love her.
Perfect—so that someone else would see a reason to value her.

She ruined herself—
losing herself
piece by piece
as she ripped them away
from her skin,
forcing herself to endure the pain
of shedding
the girl she had been

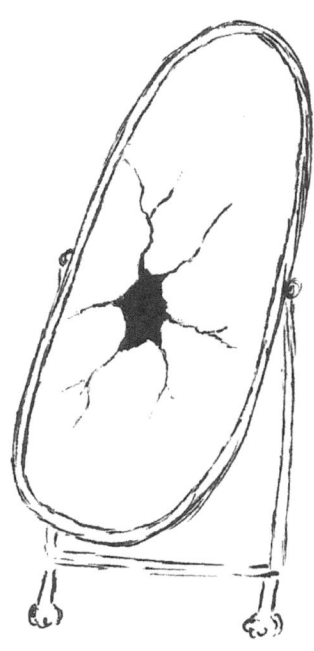

so that maybe
someone might finally
love her
for this girl
she was only
pretending to be.

I am left with scars
that I put there myself.

I am fractured along lines
and shattered like a porcelain doll
who had been dropped
from the top of the New York skyline.

I am nothing more
than a collection
of all these broken pieces.

Wren 47

I'm looking for that hand
to pull me up,
to tie me back together again,
and yet
I find no salvation
from this hollow darkness
I have fallen into
all alone.

Wren 48

Being alone
is normal,
it's true,
just no one ever confesses this
because they don't want to admit
that they were lonely too.

Wren 49

She found her only friend in the shadows,
but the shadows
always faded
no matter how she begged them to stay.

Wren 50

All she wanted
was for someone
to love the little girl
who sat all alone
at the center
of the darkness
she had covered herself with.

She wanted someone to love
the person underneath
all of her fears—
the gentle girl she hid
under the monster.

To the little girl I once was—

I'm a train wreck.
I'm an absolute mess.
I'm sorry for everything
you've gone through
and all that you haven't yet.

It doesn't get easier,
it never does,
but I hope you know
that some days
it just doesn't hurt as much.

I can't save you from the pain
and heartache
of growing up,
but know that I love you
and miss you so much.

And in the end,
I think you'll be okay,
but in truth,
I'm sorry
for all of these bad days.

-me

Wren 52

You know
how it feels
to be the last one left on shore.

You know
how it feels
to be the only passenger
waiting by the train tracks.

You know
how it feels
to be the forgotten one—
the ghost that passes by.

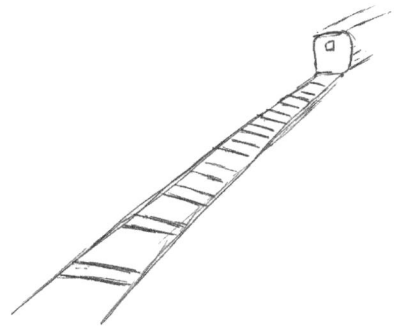

You know
the shadows
too well
to not call them home,
and so you fade
into the background
remembering
those moments
when you used to shine.

The breaking,

crying,

burning,

desperation

of trying to hold on
to something
that you were meant to let go of.

It's like begging the world to never spin
and the universe to not expand.

As if you were asking time
to halt
so that you would never have
to continue on.

Wren 54

She poured gasoline
all over her skin,
soaking her hair
and the tears fell from her eyes
and she set it all aflame
so that someone
might finally
notice her,
and yet they never did,
and so she burned alone
with the ashes,
the embers,
and the smoke
that began to coat her soul.

Wren 55

She wanted to shine,
but little did she know
just how those flames
would burn.

Wren 56

"I'm sorry I'm burning,"
She whispered to herself.

"I'm sorry the flames hurt.
I'm sorry, my dear body,
that I don't know how to make them stop."

Wren 57

Sometimes,
she thought she had begun drowning.

The air was too dense in her lungs,
filling her up with liquid
where it had once been fuel
for her dreams.

She choked on them now,
struggling
to breathe
in time
with her broken heart.

She had begun drowning, she thought,
and yet she did not know
how to find the shore
and finally pull her head
above water.

She was just a girl
born with a
perpetual smile
and an infinite sadness
that tugged at its edges.

The darkness took her hand
and led her through a waltz,
twisting her,
confusing her,
tripping her,

and so she fell,
not because she was weak,
but because she had not yet learned
how to be strong.

She was just a girl
dancing with her ghosts,
trusting
the lies
she should have hit on the head
with a baseball bat.

Wren 60

The shadows whispered to her,

"You aren't good enough."

And she believed them.

Wren 61

we're fragile creatures, beings of Broken Hearts.

Wren 62

She was still growing

"I'm here,"
She whispered
to all of those dreams
that had abandoned her.

"I'm here,"
She screamed
to the retreating backs
of all the people who left.

"I'm here,"
She mumbled
under her breath
when she watched
the world fade.

"I'm here,"
She cried
as tears fell
like a river
from her eyes
as everyone
said their goodbyes.

"I'm here,"
She shrieked
to the people
who tried to forget her.

"I'm here,"
She finally said
to the only person
who would ever matter

"I'm here,
and I'm not going anywhere,"
She announced
to the girl in the mirror.

Meet me
where I'm at.
Don't try to take my hand
and drag me along,
just hold it.
Don't try to push me forward,
I don't want to go there,
not yet.
Just stay.
For today,
just sit there beside me
and marvel at the sky
and remind me of all the beautiful things
and all of the reasons to get up tomorrow
and to try.

Wren 65

To the girl
who blows
on her plucked out
eyelashes
wishing to be beautiful—
I hope you know,
that you are so much more than that.
Whoever you are,
whatever your past,
you are who you
are meant to be—
beautiful features
and scars just the same—
and I hope you recognize
that in a world
of billions of people,
that you are the exquisite,
unique you.

So please stop
wishing
on those eyelashes
and look at all you are
instead.

Wish on her.
Count on her.
Believe in her
for she is great
if only someone
would take a chance on her,
and that person can be you.

So please,
be her.
Love her—
Love yourself.

Wren 66

When everything
wilts
and time stops,
when the wind
halts
and the sails
aren't filled.

That, darling,
is when you learn to make your own wind.
And with it,
you will go further
than someone else's wind
will ever carry you.

Wren 67

Sometimes in this life,
you have to choose the broken road.
You have to pick it for yourself,
no one else
can choose it for you.

You have to stumble down it alone,
because while it may hurt,
and while it may be scary,
it is the only way
you will ever grow
to become the person
you are meant to be.

Sometimes in life
you have to take the road that leads away.

Wren 68

It's often the lonely roads
that lead us
to who we are meant to be
because there,
we learn
how to trust our own
inner strengths.
There we begin to believe again,
not in dreams or stars,
but in the incredible potential
of our own selves.

Wren 69

You have to continue on.
Even when it gets hard,
even when you stumble.

You have to continue
so that the grass
may never grow beneath your feet.

For if you stop,
you will never grow,

you will never learn,

you will never get any further.

Wren 70

She learned
that she could not sit and dwell
on all the wrong things
for too long.

She had to keep swimming
if she ever wanted to reach
the shore.

Wren 71

The sun still sets,
even when the clouds block it from view.

You, too, must continue on,
even when no one is watching
because one day,
like the sun,
it will be your day to shine.

Wren 72

She learned that doubt
was the anchor
that tried to tie her down.

After she had spent enough time
trying to drag it around,
she finally cut it loose.

She was done
doubting
the girl she was,
but more than anything,
she was done letting that doubt
stop her
from reaching the girl she could become.

Wren 73

Sometimes you have to let it go.
If you hold on too tightly,
your sails will never fill with wind
and you'll never know
the freedom
of flying.

Wren 74

She decided then that life should not be like an
unopened notebook

left on the shelf for fear of using one of its precious pages
in a bad way.

Life should be held in your hands

and painted in

and drawn in

and written in.

Life is something that its better to fuck up trying to do right
than to never have touched at all.

Wren 75

Take back all your stars
and all your night skies.

I'm painting my own this time.

Wren 76

She knew that she was still growing up.

She still tripped

and stumbled

and fell.

But she would pick herself up

for she was still learning

and trying.

She was still growing.

Wren 77

She danced
on shards of glass.

Anger,
hate,
fear,
all of those moments
that had broken her
into so many pieces—

and even though she bled,
even though she hurt,
she kept dancing.

She knew that the moment she stopped
was the moment
they won,
and in life,
she had decided that she would be
stubborn
for herself.

She would fight for herself
and she would keep dancing
on those shards of glass
so that one day
they wouldn't hurt
anymore.

Wren 78

Don't worry about the cuts,
just keep going
and remember
that scars look pretty badass.

Wren 79

She knew she was a mess.
She knew that she wasn't perfect.

She tripped
and shattered good things
from time to time,

but she kept standing up
every time that she fell,
collecting her pieces time
and time again

because she refused
to let the failures
stop her from trying once more.

She realized
that it was okay to strive for perfection,
so long as she still loved the disaster
at the end,
regardless.

Wren 81

She was still afraid

of falling,

of failing,

of tripping,

and stumbling,

but she continued on
regardless
because she knew
that quitting
from fear
was worse
than falling again.

Wren 82

All wounds heal, just give them time.

She knew then,
what she had gotten so wrong.
She had tried to be perfect,
thinking that in perfection
was where she would become strong,

but she soon learned
that true strength came
from being able to accept the failure
and all the flaws
and continue on.

Wren 84

Learn from the broken hearts.
Learn from the failures.
Learn from the missteps.
Learn from the wrong notes.

And love, try, sing, dance again.

Wren 85

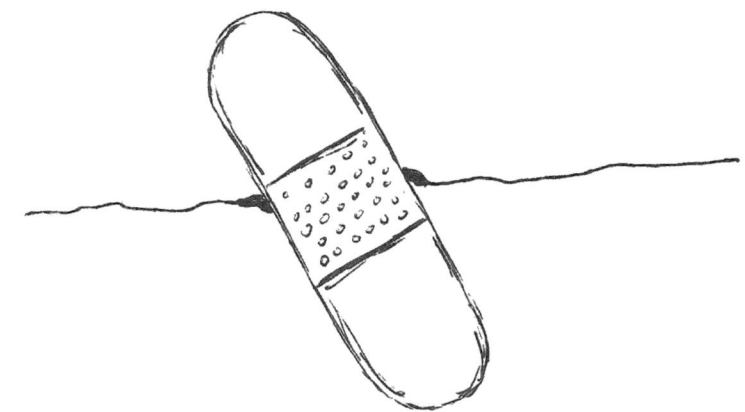

Trace your scars,
count your blessings
and thank the world for all the lessons.

Wren 86

She knew as she closed her eyes at night
that she wasn't perfect,
but this wasn't her end.

This was where she began again.
She was still becoming
the person she would be.

Wren 87

Your past
is not
your present
and
your present
is not
your future.

Wren 88

On the days that it got tough,

and she stumbled more
than she wanted to,
she reminded herself,
that one bad day
is not a bad forever,

and so she continued on
into the next day
with the hopes
that it would be better
and with the courage to continue
even if it wasn't.

Wren 89

She may have fallen,
but scraped knees
weren't the end of the world.
She had survived many times before
and she would survive many times again.

Wren 90

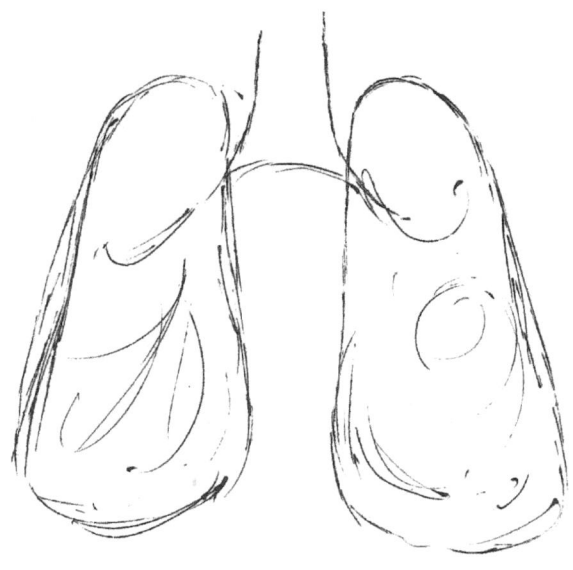

To live is to take all of the fear and the pain and continue breathing.

Wren 91

Life is surviving.

Life is rising
from the flames.

Life is becoming
in the darkness.

Life is growing
despite the weight
that tries to drag you down.

It's rough
and painful
and so hard sometimes,
but it is worth it.

Wren 92

This is where
determination bleeds into you.

This is where
you become.

This is where you fall
and this is where you will rise.

This is that moment
when you break,
and it is where you succeed.

Toe the line,
step up to the edge.

Now is your moment.
Don't run from it,
dive in.
Chase it.
Grab it and hold on so tight
that your palms bleed.

This is your life
so reach out
and take it
and never let the fear
of it slipping from your grasp
stop you from holding on
and taking it for everything
it has.

This is your moment,
so go.

Wren 93

The sun will rise,
the storm will fade,
sometimes you just have to have faith
that it will all be okay.

Wren 94

I just want someone to tell me
that it will be okay.
That everything will be okay.

Tell me,
even if it's a lie.

Tell me,
regardless of the truth
or certainty.

Just tell me
that it can't rain forever
so that I may foster
this hope inside me—

the hope
that tells me
to get back up and fight
every time
the lightning strikes me down.

Wren 95

Some times,
I think I might drown
in these tears of mine,
that fill up my world
with an ocean
of sadness,
but I'll keep swimming.

Wren 96

I hope you get your heart broken.
I hope someone breaks it a thousand times.
I hope they break it until you learn
that tears can shine.

And I hope you grow
from all of the broken pieces.
I hope you cling
tighter to the good days
and I hope you remember to smile more.
I hope you learn there is beauty in the pain,
but of all the things I hope you learn,

I hope you learn
that no matter how many times
your heart breaks,
It will keep beating
and loving
and living.

So while it may hurt more,
letting your heart be free to see the world
as it pleases
is better than locking it away in a steel cage.

It's better to feel something
than nothing at all.

People say "broken"
like it's a bad thing.

They act like mountains
weren't made from pieces of land.

They speak like they haven't valued
the pieces of sea glass they collect.

They will tell you broken is a bad thing,
but broken things are art.

Broken is where it all begins,
and aren't beginnings
beautiful?

Wren 98

You have to scream
sometimes
that "Today sucked!"

Not all days can be,
or will be, perfect,
and that is perfectly okay.
So accept it and move on

because tomorrow
could be the greatest day
yet to come.

Just promise me,
you won't ever give up.

Wren 99

Sometimes
you have to let things go
so that you can continue to grow.

Wren 100

Let the petals fall,
let the storm rain,
let yourself cry.
The only way to move on from pain
is to let it fall away.

I'll take a breath

and hold on a little tighter
and then I'll run a little farther
and then

I'll breathe again.

Wren 102

You see,
I've fallen
far too many times
to not know how
to breathe when my
ribs are broken
into pieces.

You see,
I've fallen
far too many times
to not know
how to find my feet
and stand
again.

And so you'll watch
as once more,
I rise.

Beneath the tears,
her eyes still shined.
She might have been broken,
but she was still alive.

Wren 104

I've learned
that some days,
against my better nature,

I am the damsel in distress—
the princess in the tower.

And yet,
I have also learned
that I am the knight in shining armor too,

and when I fall,
I will rescue myself.

I am in no need of
anyone else.

Wren 105

I stood then, with broken wings on my
back and taped them together.
I stitched up the tears and breaks, bandaged the
fractures and held these shoulders of mine back. I
held my head high, as if a crown rested there, like a
heavenly string pulling me up toward the clouds.

I had fallen, the dark angel to hell, but I would rise again.
And on these broken wings, and hollow winds, I
found the inner strength I never knew I had.
I found the answer to the question, "How do you
rise when you've fallen so many times?"
And I rose.

I rose as I was destined to do, on these broken wings of mine.

Wren 106

You killed me,
slowly,
terribly,
horribly.

And I didn't even notice
while you took all the air
from my lungs
or the blood from my veins.

I just smiled and pretended to be happy,
to be your happy little fool
because I was too afraid to be alone,
to not belong to you.

Eventually I even convinced myself
that this broken love
was what I deserved,
that this was how it was to be accepted.

I've learned that I deserved more—
I deserve more.

I moved on years before I reached this point,
back when I decided being alone
was better than being with you any longer,
but just now,
I've learned
I don't have to be alone.

There are people who can love me
in all the ways your selfish ego couldn't.

And so I say to you,
I'm free and I'm happy,
and that those shards of a heart you left me—

I learned how to sew into wings.

Wren 107

The song that saved me
is heavy with bass
and only meant to be blared.
It is loud
and screaming.
It is that raw breath
that rips from your lungs.

The song that saved me is not
one of grace or of finding salvation.
It is a song of damnation,
of being the dark angel
that fell from the heavens
and crashed on to earth.
It makes my heart race
and my bones rattle.

The song that saved me
was a battle cry.
It was the reminder
that reached into the depth
of my sadness
and pulled me out.
It showed me the fire
I had in me
and it forced me to take it.

The song that saved me
is not pretty.
It is raw.
It is me
learning to stand again.
It is me
finding these words
and finally screaming.

Growth isn't easy
or beautiful.
It is real
and raging,
and so, horribly raw.

Wren 108

I stood
at the edge of the waves
and watched them crash.

The wind blew
my hair across my face
as the grey skies darkened
and the boats anchored into place.

The storm was coming
and I was learning
how to not
be afraid.

In the loneliness
and in the abyss,
she found herself.

And so she pulled herself
from the bottomless pit—
finding her feet beneath her,
she rose like a warrior,

despite the way her hands shook,

despite the way her heart beat so unsteadily,

despite the way she was still afraid.

She rose
because that was what she was destined to do.

Wren 110

She followed her dreams
no matter how people spit on her and her imagination
because she didn't need their love.

All that mattered to her
in that moment before she closed her eyes
was whether or not she loved herself.

♡

Wren 111

It doesn't take perfect conditions
or a garden to grow a daisy.

Sometimes,
just a small crack in the universe
is enough for something beautiful to bloom.

Wren 112

She continued on

one step
after another.

She continued on

she stumbled,
she rose,
she danced,
and she crawled.

She continued on

through the dark days
and the good ones too.

She continued on

because she knew that at the end of the day
each step she took
was another one,
no matter how small
or how big,
toward her dreams.

She continued on

because she was still growing,
still off in search
of whatever great thing that came next.

Eventually She would bloom

She was not perfect—
She had scars on her hands she didn't remember getting
and hair that curled in all the wrong ways.
She was a mess most days,
but it was her life
and she wouldn't change it.
So no,
She wasn't perfect—
not by your definition of the word,
but by hers.

Wren 115

She laughed

at the people
who told her
she looked insane,
as if she hadn't slept in days
and ran her life
like she was
a recovering psychopath,
for she didn't care
for their opinions.

Why did it matter
what they thought of her
when all the love she needed
could be found in herself?

Wren 116

She decided she wouldn't let the world change her.
She decided that she would be true to herself—
her perfectly unfiltered, unpolished, beautiful self—

or she would be no one at all.

She was a thousand broken things
twisted and stitched together
into something beautifully whole.

In the mirror,
she looked at the piece of fabric
she called her skin
and she traced her battle scars,
counting the wars
and the cuts she gained along the way—

The wounds on her heart,
the scrapes on her elbows,
the cuts on her hands and on the bottoms of her feet—

every scar,
every tear,

a story burned
into the fabric of her being,

reminding her
that against all odds,
she had survived.

I am an artist
of many failed masterpieces
and a runner
with a twisted knee.

I am a dancer
with a broken foot
and a poet
of many failed decrees.

I am nothing to the universe,
but I am everything to me.

Wren 120

She was different.
She played the same game,
but knew different rules.
She smiled at strangers,
but frowned at them too.

She was different.
She was a stranger to all,
but a friend to many.
She was a princess,
but she was also a dragon.
She would burn,
but calm and contained,
not like a wildfire.

She was different,
but she was grand.
She was different,
but she was beautiful.
She was different,
but she was exactly who she needed to be.

Wren 121

Her hands no longer shook
in the ways they used to.

Her legs no longer felt weak
as she stood up for herself.

And when it came to her heart,
it was calm and controlled.

She had grown
to fit the armor
bestowed upon her,
and now she would challenge
the world.

She wore her weakness
like armor
and challenged the world
to a fight.

At the end of the day,
when she stripped away
all of the ornamentation
and honors
and awards
and looked herself in the eye,
she smiled
knowing the girl beneath it all
was the best prize.

Every time I walk past my reflection in a mirror,
I smile a little more,
taking in everything that I am—
every scar,
every broken feature,
every roll of fat,
and I love myself a little more
because that girl in the mirror
is courageous,
and kind,
and smart,
and beautiful in her soul,
and that is far more important
than appearing pretty in a piece of glass.

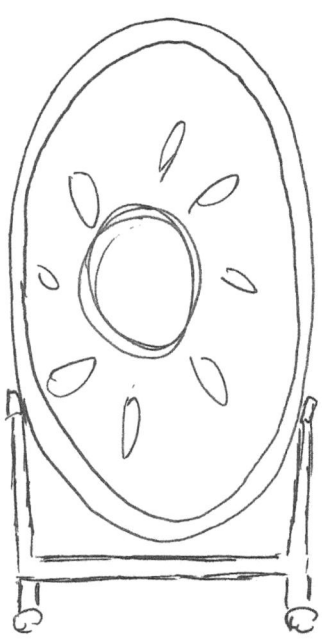

Everyday,
I say "I love you"
to the girl in the mirror,
and everyday she says it back.

And I smile because there is nothing
like the feeling of true love
born inside your own heart
that will always
be reciprocated.

To younger me:

I know she's not the girl you dreamed of,
and she's not the one you asked for,
but you'll be proud of her.
You'll love her,
because she's so much more.

-me

Wren 127

The sun sets
on another beautiful day
and I feel the soft beating of my full heart
and I breathe the cold fall air into my lungs.

As I do, I am reminded of that little girl
who dreamed of someone like me,
that little girl who would be proud,
and I take her pride
and I stand a little taller.

She laughed
then for the little girl
she loved.

The little girl
she knew once—
the little girl
she was.

The one
who had never dreamed of
princesses or of being the girl in the tower.

The one who had instead dreamed
of being her own hero,
made of fire,
who fought crime
and saved herself
each time.

She had become her—
that girl
she had dreamed of.

She had become
the girl of fire
and she saved herself.

She would have loved to say
that she had conquered all of her fears,
but she wasn't one for lying.

She was still afraid,
but she kept going,
persevering
into the great unknown
that lay before her
so that one day

that "great unknown"
would not be so big.

Wren 130

Many people told me to stop—
stop trying so hard,
stop running so far,
stop caring,
but I didn't.

See, they wanted me to stop
for their own benefit,
but for myself,
and for my future
and the little girl who dreamed of greatness,

I kept trying
and I kept caring
and I kept running
and eventually,
I left them
in the dust.

As I stood there,
on the edge of a beautiful tomorrow,
watching the sun rise above the horizon,
painting the sky a pastel pink,

I realized that I had one shot at this life
and I could use it to be either loved
by people who didn't want to see me succeed,
or hated by people who envied me for following
and achieving my dreams.

And as the sun rose
fully into view,
I realized then,
as you should too,
that your life
will only ever be truly lived
by you
being you.

Wren 132

My eyes crinkle at the edges
from a life well worn.

I am the ashes that have fallen,
I am the fading remnants of the storm.

I have lived
and now I lie
here at the end,

where beginnings begin
and endings end

watching as the sun sets
but knowing that on the other side
it will now rise.

Wren 133

What people said
couldn't be done,
she did.
Just to say
that the impossible
is always possible
if only one
has enough faith
to believe
in the power
of themselves.

People watch her
the way they watch the sun
as it rises and sets,
watching something uniquely beautiful
take place in front of them
with burning envy
and a silent admiration.

It's golden where I stand now,
but looking back on the darker days,
I always start to say, "What a waste of some good days,"
but then I stop
because as hard to admit as it is,
I needed those darker days
to make me the way I am
so that I could find the golden place
on which I now stand.

Sometimes, you just have to laugh,
sometimes that's all you can do.
In a world where we remain so powerless,
when you're afraid
or elated,
or anything in between,
all you can ever do is laugh.

Because look at where you came from—
look at the beginning of the trail,
and look at where you have gotten yourself.
Look at everything you have struggled with,
look at everything you failed
and look at everything you won.
Look at how you conquered it all,
and you—you, yourself and you,
carried yourself here,

to today.

To this moment.

And no matter what this life throws at you,
know that you have come so very far.
And that when it gets too hard,
just remember everything and laugh,
be joyful.
This life is a storm,
but your boat has sailed through.

So, laugh.
Because you survived
and sometimes,
that is all you can do.

Wren 137

She smiled at the sun.
The storm was finally gone.
She had sailed through
and the victorious feeling that swelled in her chest
had far more power than
a thousand bad nights combined.

She had survived.

And I lived happily ever after in my chaos and my crazy,
with all I could ever need a part of me,

knowing that I was still, and always, growing.

Wren 139

About the Author

Wren is just an ordinary teenage girl from a little town in the corner of nowhere. She is inspired by the grief and the pain of living as well as the beauty of the journey. She hopes that others may read her words and feel a little less alone in the process that is growing up. She believes that tomorrow is another chance to try again, and that no matter how hard it gets, you must keep going because eventually the sun will rise. *Still Growing* is her first collection of poetry.

Follow her on Instagram @poetwren or
visit her website www.poetwren.com

www.ingramcontent.com/pod-product-compliance
Lightning Source LLC
Chambersburg PA
CBHW051629120626

46551CB00014B/1995